Phantoms and Footie

Mind Your Own Business
by Gillian Cross 3
Illustrated by Leonie Shearing

Jack the Lad
by Jean Ure 21
Illustrated by David Whittle

The Door
by Gareth Owen 41
Illustrated by Alan Marks

Rigby is an imprint of Pearson Education Limited, a company
incorporated in England and Wales, having its registered office at
Edinburgh Gate, Harlow, Essex, CM20 2JE.
Registered company number: 872828
www.rigbyed.co.uk

Rigby is a registered trademark of Reed Elsevier Inc, Licensed to
Pearson Education Limited

Fire, Phantoms and Footie first published 2002

'Mind Your Own Business' © Gillian Cross 2002
'Jack the Lad' © Jean Ure 2002
'The Door' © Gareth Owen 2002

Series editor: Wendy Wren

10
12 11

| *Fire, Phantoms and Footie* | ISBN 978 0433 07801 2 |
| Group Reading Pack with Teaching Notes | ISBN 978 0433 07807 4 |

Illustrated by Leonie Shearing, David Whittle, Alan Marks
Cover illustration © Tokay Interactive Ltd 2002
Repro by Digital Imaging, Glasgow
Printed in China (CTPS/11)

MIND YOUR OWN BUSINESS

by Gillian Cross

Alec could see Phil and Matt laughing at him, from inside the bus. His mother was running after him, waving his heavy old raincoat.

"You forgot this!" she said.

"I don't want a mac," Alec growled.

"You'll need it up on the hills."

His mother bundled the mac into his backpack and Alec pulled a face and scrambled on to the bus. He scuttled into the last seat – next to Laura and right in front of Phil and Matt.

"Scared of getting wet?" Phil jeered.

Matt ruffled Alec's hair. "We'll soon dry you off."

He and Phil sniggered and there was an odd little rattling noise. Alec glanced round to see what they'd got, but their eyes were cold, warning him off. *Mind your own business.* He turned back, fast, and looked out of the window instead.

The view wasn't very interesting. All he could see was grey sky and endless fields. By the time the bus pulled into the car park at Blacklow Ridge, he was bored and restless, like everyone else.

He wasn't expecting the steep ridge that rose abruptly on the far side of the car park. Laura gasped when she saw it, and even Phil was impressed. "We'll need ropes to get up there, Miss."

"Nonsense," Miss Newbold said briskly. "It's just a stroll."

She lined them up in the car park, putting them into groups and handing out worksheets. The hard-working people went into her group, of course. They all adored her. Some of the girls were even wearing shorts, to copy her.

Miss Newbold beamed at them. "It's a circular walk. You'll be coming along the ridge with me this morning and going back down through the wood this afternoon. Mr Sohal's group will do it the other way round. And we'll all meet at the beacon for lunch."

She set off across the car park to the steps that climbed gently up the ridge. Her group streamed after her, clutching clipboards and chattering excitedly.

Mr Sohal looked round at the assortment of villains and dawdlers left behind. "Come on, you lot."

A few people groaned, but no one moved.

"What's the beacon?" asked Laura.

"It's the stone tower on top of the ridge," said Mr Sohal. "They used to light bonfires there. Now let's get going."

Who lit bonfires? Alec wondered. *Why?* But Mr Sohal wasn't saying any more. He nodded at Mary Cable's mum, who always came to help on trips. Mrs Cable trudged off down towards the wood and the group trailed after her, with Mr Sohal at the back, hassling the stragglers.

The wood was dim and soggy and boring. Mrs Cable kept trying to get everyone interested in their worksheets.

"There's a holly!" she said eagerly. "And that's an alder! You can tick those off."

Phil yawned.

Mrs Cable tried again. "I know! Let's collect a leaf from each kind of tree!"

That looked like falling flat too – until Matt suddenly grinned. "Yeah!" he said. "Let's collect stuff."

That acted like a signal. Everyone cheered. Then they plunged off the path, scattering into the wood.

"Come back!" yelled Mr Sohal. "Get back on the path!"

No one took any notice. Mr Sohal and Mrs Cable began chasing after people, trying to chivvy them back to the path. The whole wood was in an uproar.

Alec hadn't gone very far when he glanced back and saw Matt and Phil, still on the path. They were just strolling along and talking. Every now and again – when Mr Sohal and Mrs Cable weren't looking – they bent down quickly and scooped something up.

Alec watched, out of the corner of his eye.

First, Matt picked something up and slipped it into Phil's backpack. Then Phil did the same, dropping his find into Matt's bag. What were they doing?

"Wood," said Laura suddenly, from behind Alec's right ear.

Alec jumped. "Wood?"

"Sticks." Laura nudged him as Phil bent down again. Alec had a glimpse of pale bark and jagged, snapped wood. Then the sticks went into Matt's backpack, with the top flapped over to hide them. When Mr Sohal glanced round a second later, there was nothing to see except the two boys walking along with their hands in their pockets.

"They're up to something." Laura sounded scared.

Alec remembered how they'd stared at him on the bus. "It's none of our business," he said nervously.

Laura didn't argue. But she kept watching.

By the time they reached the far end of the wood, Matt and Phil both had bulging backpacks. But no one else noticed. They were too busy groaning about the next bit of path.

"It's *vertical!*"

"We'll *die!*"

The ridge was much higher at this end and the path zigzagged all the way to the top.

Laura went pale. "It's very steep," she said.

Alec remembered about her asthma. "Don't worry," he said. "I'll go up with you."

They went slowly, but Laura was wheezing badly by the time they reached the top. Alec thought it would get easier then, but he was wrong. As the ground levelled, the trees stopped abruptly and the path led out on to the open ridge.

They stepped out of the wood and the wind hit them head-on, almost knocking Laura over. Alec grabbed her arm to hold her steady.

Everyone was yelling.

"It's not fair! We'll be walking back into the wind."

"The others had it behind them!"

"And they'll be going *down* the zigzags. It's not fair!"

The beacon was just ahead, a round, squat tower, with no door. The wind roared past it, and the only shelter was close by the walls. But Miss Newbold's group was already there. They'd taken all the sheltered places.

"You should walk faster!" Miss Newbold called brightly. "We've been here for twenty minutes!"

She hardly gave them time to eat their sandwiches before she started handing out the afternoon's worksheets, pushing them impatiently at people who dithered.

"Come on, Laura. Take your sheet."

Laura was tired and her fingers fumbled. Miss Newbold thrust a worksheet at her – and loosened her grip on the others.

Instantly, the wind whisked them out of her hand. Pieces of paper whipped past Alec's face, swirling into the trees and snagging on branches.

Matt and Phil glanced at each other and jumped up.

"Don't worry, Miss Newbold!"

"We'll get them!"

Racing back into the wood, they began collecting the sheets, jumping for the ones caught on high branches. Some of the sheets tore, and Phil pushed those hastily into his pocket.

"Paper too," Laura said faintly, from somewhere near Alec's feet. "They've got paper *and* wood." She sounded even more scared now.

Alec almost asked her why. But Miss Newbold suddenly started talking again, waving her arms around. "This is only a token, but it might help you to imagine the real bonfire … "

Opening her backpack, she took out a big, fat candle. *Groan*, thought Alec, forgetting about Laura. He knew what was coming. Miss Newbold was going to light the candle and tell them to pretend it was a huge bonfire. She was always doing things like that. 'Imagining', she called it. Tomorrow they'd do a 'creative writing' exercise about it. *Groan*.

Miss Newbold put the candle on the ground and pulled a box of matches out of her backpack. Bending down, she lit a match. It blew out straight away. So did the second one. With a cross little laugh, she struck a third match.

As that blew out, Matt and Phil came back with all the worksheets they'd managed to reach.

They saw the matches and glanced at each other again, very quickly.

Matt said, "Here, Miss. We'll give you a hand."

He picked up the candle and moved it back, standing it right against the beacon, almost out of the wind. Phil snatched the matches out of Miss Newbold's hand. He and Matt knelt down on either side of the candle, shielding it with their bodies, and Alec heard a match scrape against the box. There was a pause.

Then Phil said, "There you are, Miss."

He and Matt stood up. The candle was burning steadily in the shelter of the beacon.

Miss Newbold caught her breath. "That's *lovely*." She half-closed her eyes and started to murmur. "I want you all to imagine ... "

Alec tried. He looked at the candle and tried to pretend it was a huge blaze. But all he saw was a little thread of flame – with Phil behind it, holding the matchbox over Miss Newbold's backpack.

Phil gave the box a little shake and dropped it into the backpack – and Alec went cold. As he heard the matches rattle, he recognised the noise he'd heard on the bus.

Phil and Matt had wood and paper – and matches.

They wouldn't dare, he thought.

In front of him, Miss Newbold was crooning on. " ... Imagine giant flames, shooting into the sky, and showers of sparks, flying upwards ... "

Phil and Matt bent over the candle, grinning at each other. *They wouldn't dare*, Alec thought again. *Not even them.*

It looked as though he was right. Once the candle was out, they all started to pack up. Phil and Matt bundled up their sandwich wrappers and put on their backpacks, just like everyone else.

"See you at the bus!" Miss Newbold said jauntily.

She and her group turned away to walk down the zigzag path into the wood.

Mr Sohal looked round at the rest of them and sighed, "Right, let's get going."

With a chorus of moans, they heaved themselves off the ground and began battling forwards, into the wind. Laura had to cling on to Mrs Cable for support and Alec could tell she was wheezing already.

They'd been going for almost five minutes when Matt suddenly stopped.

"Oh no!" he yelled.

Mr Sohal looked round. "What's up?"

"I've left my CD Walkman by the beacon!" Matt shook his head. "My mum'll kill me! She's only just bought it."

"Run back then, you stupid boy," Mr Sohal said wearily. "We'll stay here and do the worksheet."

Matt shot off instantly – and so did Phil.

Mr Sohal shrugged. "I hope the exercise does them good. Sit down everyone. Let's get this worksheet out of the way."

Phil and Matt were half-way to the beacon now, running with the wind behind them. Alec watched their backpacks bumping up and down against their shoulders and thought, *They can't be going to do it. They CAN'T.*

Laura shuffled over to him. Her eyes were wide. "They've got matches too," she whispered. "I heard them, on the bus."

"So?" Alec was still trying to mind his own business. "They lit fires there in the olden days, didn't they? If it was OK then— "

"But the wind!" Laura looked as if she wanted to shake him. "Don't you *see?* The *wind!*"

Why did the wind matter, Alec thought impatiently. *What difference—* ?

Then Laura pointed and he saw what she meant. The wind was blowing straight towards the wood – straight towards Miss Newbold's group. "If the wind blows sparks into the trees— " said Alec.

"The whole wood could burn!" Laura said.

Matt and Phil had reached the beacon now and disappeared behind it. Alec sighed. "OK. I'll tell Mr Sohal."

"Make him go to the beacon!" Laura said.

Alec struggled to his feet, and battled his way over to Mr Sohal and Mrs Cable. "Phil and Matt have gone to start a fire!" he shouted.

Mr Sohal looked up placidly.

"It's all right. Phil put the matches back in Miss Newbold's bag. I was watching."

"Yeah, that's right!"

Everyone started joining in.

"He dropped them in."

"Anyway, there's nothing to burn."

"You need fuel for a fire."

Alec looked round for Laura. He needed someone to back him up.

But Laura wasn't there.

While he was talking, she'd scrambled up and set off for the beacon, running as fast as she could. She was twenty metres away already. Running towards the beacon.

What on Earth—?

Then Alec remembered what she'd said. *Make him go to the beacon!* That was what she was doing. She wanted Mr Sohal to go after her.

It was a good idea, but she was never going to make it to the tower. She staggered in the wind and then stopped short, doubling over to cough. Alec realised that there was only one way to get Mr Sohal to the beacon in time.

He turned round and ran, with his backpack thudding against his back.

As he passed Laura, she pointed ahead, still coughing. There was a thin thread of smoke billowing out from behind the beacon now. And a stream of sparks, caught by the wind. Alec put his head down and ran harder.

He was almost there when Matt and Phil stepped out from behind the tower.
Mind your own business, their faces said.

But this is my business! Alec thought. *It's everyone's business!*

He kept going, charging straight at them. They tried to block his way, but he had the full force of the wind behind him. He blasted through, racing round to the back of the beacon.

The flames were as high as his waist. The crumpled worksheets from Phil's pocket were blazing at the heart of the heap, and the dry wood piled round them was crackling and spitting as it started to burn. Even in the shelter of the tower, there was enough wind to send a stream of sparks whirling away towards the trees.

Alec launched himself at the pile of sticks, kicking it to bits.

His trainers blackened and scorched. Matt and Phil tried to pull him away, but he didn't stop kicking, until the wood was all scattered with its red glow dwindling into an ashy grey.

When he was sure the fire was safe, he spun round to yell at Matt and Phil, but he never got the words out. He had seen the flames in the trees behind them.

There were bits of paper lodged in the branches – worksheets that Matt and Phil hadn't managed to reach earlier. The sparks had set those on fire and they were blazing hard. In a few moments the whole wood could be burning. And Miss Newbold's group was down there somewhere.

Matt and Phil gave a gasp, but Alec had no time to waste on them. Racing to the edge of the wood, he yelled as loudly as he could.

"FIRE! FIRE!"

It was useless. The wind blew his voice away, over the tops of the trees.

Looking back, he saw Mr Sohal and Mrs Cable coming, but they weren't near enough to help. All the paper was burning fiercely now and some of the twigs around it were starting to smoke. *I can't reach it!* Alec thought. *I can't do anything!*

Then he remembered his mac.

Wrenching his backpack open, he pulled it out.

Holding it by one corner, he flapped it as hard as he could, beating at the flames. The mac tangled round twigs and snagged on branches, but he tore it free and went on flapping, jumping to reach higher and stamping out the burning paper that fell to the ground.

He was almost collapsing from exhaustion when Mr Sohal and Mrs Cable reached him. Mrs Cable snatched the mac from him and beat out the rest of the flames, high above his head. Mr Sohal kicked dust over the smouldering branches and took a firm hold on Matt and Phil.

When the last flame was out, Mrs Cable, still clutching the mac, turned to Alec. "You're something," she said. "You're quite something, Alec Maclean."

"It wasn't me," Alec said. "It was Laura."

He looked past the beacon and waved at her, to let her know it was all right. She straightened up and waved back, grinning.

And Alec picked up his filthy, tattered mac and thought, *Mum's going to kill me!*

* * *

But she didn't. When Mr Sohal finished telling her the story, she was very quiet for a moment. Then she looked up triumphantly at Alec. "I told you you'd need a mac on those hills!" she said.

Jack the Lad

by Jean Ure

"I dare you!" said Tara.

"Dare you back!" said Sally.

"You first! I dared first!"

Sally hesitated. She looked at the pond, inky black beneath its layer of ice. Then she looked back at the house, with its brightly lit sign: Diamond Academy of Drama. Mr Diamond would be there, in the studio. Shayna, Dee, and the others would all be arriving.

"Well, go on!" said Tara. "What are you waiting for?"

Still Sally hesitated. They had been told repeatedly not to go on the ice, and Sally was, on the whole, the sort of person who did as she was told.

"I knew you were too chicken!" jeered Tara.

"I'm not," said Sally. "But we'll be late for class!"

"Not if you just get on with it!"

It was only a small pond, though it was deep in the middle. Deep as an ocean, someone had said. But one quick dash and she would be across!

Sally took a breath. "All right," she said.

Just one quick dash ... then suddenly, **CRACK!** The ice split apart and Sally went tumbling through. She had time for just one panic-stricken gasp before the water closed over her head. Terror cut her like a knife. Frantically, she thrashed out with arms and legs, clawed in desperation at the edges of the hole; but the ice broke in chunks, her fingers scrabbled in vain and slid back, into the water. And Sally went plunging down.

And oh, it was cold! So cold!

* * *

Sally was floating. But she wasn't floating in water. She was floating in the air! This was very strange. It was also rather disturbing. She didn't feel at all her usual self. She felt … weightless. She felt … bodiless! *Help, help!* Where was her body?

Sally looked down. Her body was there – but she could see right through it! She could see a little group of people, gathered by the pool. Tara, Mr Diamond, Shayna and Dee; Ryan Biggs, Rory McGibbon. Mr Diamond was bending over something – or someone – lying on the grass. The others were watching. What were they doing down there? What was Sally doing up here?

She jumped as she saw a finger suddenly shoot out of nowhere and prod her. She couldn't feel it, but she could see it going in and out. A voice spoke in her ear, "Oy!"

Sally spun round. A boy was hovering by her left shoulder. A boy with a cheeky face and sandy hair and cheeks full of freckles. Just like Sally herself, he was completely transparent! She could make out the shape of him, but he wasn't *solid*. Not at all like a body ought to be.

Sally gulped. Something very creepy was going on …

"W–Who are you?" she asked.

"I'm Jack," said the boy. He did a little prance, in mid-air. "Jack the Lad! Mad and bad! Who are you?"

"I'm S–Sally," said Sally.

"I never seen you before! How long you been here?"

Sally swallowed. "Um … about a minute, I should think."

"Oh! You're new," said Jack. "Don't worry! You'll soon get used to it."

"Get used to w–what?" said Sally.

"Being a ghost."

Sally felt rather frightened. A bit indignant too. "I'm not a ghost!" How could she be a ghost? You had to be dead to be a ghost!

"You are," said Jack. "You just don't realise it. Takes a bit of time. Took me a while. How did you die? I fell through the ice and got drowned. Is that what happened to you?" he asked, cosily.

Sally struggled with a faint, uncomfortable memory – Mr Diamond telling them, "On no account are you to go on the ice. It's not safe." Then Tara, taunting her, "I dare you! I dare you! I knew you were chicken!"

Sally gave a little squeak of panic and dropped to the ground.

"Mr Diamond!" she shouted. "Shayna! Dee!"

"That won't do any good," said Jack, zooming down beside her. "They can't hear you … They can't even see you. That's you, lying on the ground. You're dead! You're a ghost!"

"I can't be!" wailed Sally. "I'm going to London next week!"

The pupils of the Diamond Academy had reached the finals of the Schools' Drama Competition, and Sally was playing the leading role. She had been looking forward to it for weeks. Oh, how could she have been so stupid? Ruining her chances, just for a dare! Just to show Tara … In one mad moment she had thrown her entire life away. And then there was Mum. Poor Mum! And Dad! How were they going to feel?

"You'll soon find your feet," said Jack. He sniggered. "Find your feet … That's a joke! You're meant to laugh."

"Well," said Sally. "It's not funny. I've ruined my life! I *was* going to go to London!"

"I'd give anything to go to London," said Jack. His eyes gleamed. "If I went to London I could visit the King!"

"What *king*?" said Sally, crossly.

Jack strutted. "King George, of course!"

"It isn't King George," said Sally. "It's the Queen."

"Qu–Queen?" For the first time, Jack faltered.

"Queen *Elizabeth*," said Sally. "The second," she added, just to make sure.

Jack frowned. "How long has she been there?"

"I don't know. Since before I was born. Since before my mum was born. For ever!" said Sally.

"Oh, well! That's all right." Jack did a little bounce. "I could go and visit *her*. I could haunt her in her palace! I could take off my head and tuck it under my arm."

Sally's eyes widened as Jack's head suddenly disappeared and then popped up again beneath his right armpit.

"I could go and moan in her bedroom! I could throw the royal hairbrushes about! I could rattle the windows! I could— "

"Stop it!" said Sally. "And put your head back on. It makes me feel sick!"

"You could take yours off if you wanted," said Jack.

"Well, I don't," said Sally. "And as for going to London to frighten the Queen, that's the meanest thing I've ever heard!"

"I wouldn't frighten her," said Jack. He tossed his head in the air and caught it as it came down. "I'd make her laugh!"

"You'd make her *sick*," said Sally.

Jack sighed. He put his head back where it belonged. "I just want to be where there are people," he said. "There aren't any people round here! You're the first person I've talked to since I got drowned. I'm lonely!" wailed Jack. "I don't want to be on my own any more!"

"I don't understand," said Sally. "If you're a ghost, why can't you just get up and … ghost off somewhere?"

"It doesn't work like that. You have to have someone to help you. Like, for instance," said Jack, "if you were *really* going to London, you could take me with you."

Sally opened her mouth to say, "I am really going to London!" But then, instead, she found herself saying, "How could I do that?"

"Easy," said Jack. "I could transfer myself to – to that bit of pebble, say." He pointed at a small pink pebble lying by the side of the pond. "I could make my spirit enter the pebble, then you could pick it up and put it in your pocket, and carry it off, and I could come with you. Then you could take me to Buckingham Palace and leave me in a corner, and I could stay there for ever and ever and have *fun!* But I can't do it by myself. You'd have to take me. And you can't," said Jack, "'cos you're *dead*, you're lying there *dead*, and now you'll be stuck here same as me and we'll never get away!"

"That's not true!" screamed Sally. Ryan Biggs had just stepped back and she had caught a glimpse of herself, stretched out on the ground. "I'm not dead!"

Sally raced across the grass and gave Ryan Biggs a mighty shove. Ryan didn't even notice! Sally had run right through him ...

"See? I told you," said Jack. "You're dead."

"I'm not! I'm not!" Sally ran distractedly to and fro. From Dee to Shayna to Mr Diamond. "Please hear me! Please tell me it's not true! I'm here! I'm alive! Somebody please ... "

* * *

Sally felt as if she were floating. Floating somewhere ... white! Lots of white! White all round her. Everywhere she looked. White ... and soft. She was lying on something. A bed! With her head on a ... pillow! She had arms – and legs – and a body!

Cautiously, Sally let her right arm wander up into the air. She gazed at it. It was definitely an arm. She let it fall back again. It landed with a satisfying 'flump' on the pillow. There it lay, firm and solid, just the way an arm ought to be.

Why was she so relieved? How else would an arm feel?

Sally wasn't sure; but somewhere at the back of her mind she had a vague memory of being able to see right through herself – of talking to a boy who claimed to be a ghost. Who had said that *she* was a ghost ...

"Sally?"

Sally turned her head on the pillow. Her mum and dad were standing there, both looking as real and as solid as could be.

"Mum! I'm not a ghost, am I?"

Mum hugged her and said, "No, darling, you're not a ghost!"

"Then where am I?" whispered Sally.

Mum told her that she was in hospital. "You gave us such a fright!"

"How much do you remember?" asked Dad.

"Just … falling through the ice," said Sally. She wasn't sure of the rest. Whether it had been a dream or whether it was real.

"You know that you were unconscious?" said Dad.

Unconscious! So maybe it had just been a dream? But she had seen Mr Diamond and all the others gathered round her body.

Dad took her hand. "You don't need me to tell you that what you did was extremely stupid."

Sally turned her head away. "It wasn't my fault! It was Tara. She dared me!"

Dad said, "Now Sally! What kind of excuse is that? Are you telling me that you don't have a mind of your own?"

"Of course she does!" said Mum. She looked very sternly at Sally. "I honestly don't feel that you deserve to go to London."

"Mum! Please!" begged Sally. "It's really important!"

"A pity you didn't think of that sooner," said Mum; but Dad said that he thought Sally had learned her lesson – sometimes he was a bit softer than Mum.

"I think we can trust her."

"Well, all right," said Mum, "but I'm afraid you won't be able to attend the last few rehearsals, so I don't know what Mr Diamond is going to say. He might have to ask you to play a smaller part."

It was a horrible thought, but Mum said she would have to be prepared for it. "Every action has its consequences."

After Mum and Dad had left the hospital, Sally lay there with her brain buzzing like a beehive. She thought, *Jack. Pebble. Smaller part! Buckingham Palace. Smaller part! Haunt the Queen. Smaller part! Take me to London. Smaller part!* And then it was Dee and Shayna's turn to visit, and just for a while the buzzing ceased.

"We thought you were dead," said Dee. "We thought you'd been drowned!"

"Your heart had stopped," said Shayna. "If Tara hadn't run for help, it would have been too late!"

Sally scowled. She didn't want to hear about Tara.

"I could still see you all," she said. "I saw you all standing there."

"Wow!" breathed Shayna. "An out-of-body experience!"

"What was it like?" Dee wanted to know.

"It was ... weird," said Sally. And that was all she would tell them.

It wasn't until Sally went back for the final rehearsal that Mr Diamond broke the bad news to her.

"I'm so sorry, Sally! I've had to change the parts around."

Sally was now going to say *two lines* and act as understudy. Her part had been given to ... Tara Philpott!

"*Poor* Sally," crooned Tara. "I feel *so* guilty. I'm sure she would have done it ever so much better than I will!"

"Some people think you should have got the part in the first place," simpered Martina Jones.

"*No!*" Tara fluttered her lashes and turned coyly pink. "Surely not?"

Sally wandered glumly out into the garden. She shivered as she looked at the pond. She didn't ever want to go near it again!

She was about to turn back indoors when a small, faint, far-away voice plaintively echoed in her ear: "Sallee … help me!"

"J–Jack?" said Sally.

Jack the Lad. Drowned in an icy pool. Poor Jack! He had been so lost and lonely, all by himself. He had also been unbearably full of himself and *totally inconsiderate*. If, of course, he had really existed. If Sally hadn't just been dreaming.

"*Sallee* … help me!"

She could still be dreaming, even now. There weren't such things as ghosts were there?

But just in case ... thought Sally.

Gingerly, Sally crept forward to the edge of

the pool. Feeling rather stupid, she reached down and picked up the pebble. Shell-pink; the one Jack had pointed to.

"Jack, if you're there," she whispered, "I'll take you to London!"

* * *

Strange things happened on the train. One was Sally's can of coke up-ending itself all over Martina Jones' head. How could that have happened? Another was the strap of Sally's bag suddenly snaking out into the gangway just as Tara Philpott was walking past. How could *that* have happened? Sally hadn't made her fall over! But she got the blame.

"You did that on purpose!" hissed Tara.

"She doesn't want you to be in the play!" shrieked Martina.

Mr Diamond looked cross and said, "Haven't you caused enough trouble, Sally?"

Sally felt very humiliated. She went into the corridor and took the little pink pebble out of her pocket. Could it really contain Jack's spirit? She addressed it, sternly.

"Jack, if that's you," she said, "I wish you would stop it! Can you hear me? Stop it!"

And somewhere near her left ear came a little cackle of laughter.

"*Jack?*" said Sally.

This was too much! She had rescued a ghost, and now it wouldn't behave itself. All the way to London, Jack was on the move, darting here and there about the carriage, throwing people's bags to the floor, tugging at their hair, dropping things on their feet.

Mr Diamond said, "I just don't know what the matter is with you today, Sally. Why are you so hyper?" Tara sniggered, and so did Martina Jones.

By the time they reached their hotel, Sally was just about sick of it. She was beginning to wish she had left Jack behind.

"Go and bother *her*!" she said, and she slipped the little pink pebble into Tara's pocket …

In the middle of the night, the guests of the Briarley Hotel were woken by the sound of terrible screeching. Sally, Dee and Shayna were sharing a room. They all sprang up, in a panic.

"W–what is it?" quavered Shayna.

Sally clutched at her bedclothes. "S–sounds like s–someone's being m–murdered!"

Dee, who was the bravest, got out of bed and went to look. After a moment of hesitation, Sally tiptoed after her. Shayna stayed where she was, ready to dive back under the duvet.

Slowly, Dee edged the door open just a crack. As she did so, Tara ran past, screaming. She was followed by Martina, also screaming.

All around, doors were opening, heads were popping out. Sally, growing bold, crept into the corridor. From where she stood, she could see into the room that Tara and Martina were sharing. It was **A MESS.** Clothes had been tossed all over the floor. A bag had been emptied. A chair had been thrown over. A pair of tights hung from the curtain rail.

"What on *Earth*—?" gasped Mr Diamond.

"It's a ghost!" shrieked Tara, hurling herself at the stairs. "It's a poltergeist!"

This time, no one could say that it was Sally's fault when Tara tripped over and fell headfirst down to the next landing. But Sally knew who was responsible!

"Jack?" She whispered it, accusingly. "Is that you?"

The only reply was a ghostly chuckle from somewhere up near the ceiling. Nobody seemed to hear it except Sally.

The next day, Tara was still feeling shaky, and her left wrist was swollen.

"It looks as if Sally will have to play the lead role after all," said Mr Diamond.

Sally gulped. She would have liked

nothing better than to take over – but was it quite fair? She hadn't meant Tara to fall down the stairs!

"I won't do it if you don't want me to," she said to Tara. "I could always tell Mr Diamond I can't remember the lines."

"Are you mad?" screeched Tara. "How can I act with a sprained wrist?"

I would, thought Sally. *I'd act if I had two sprained wrists*. But Tara said she couldn't possibly.

It was up to Sally!

"If you don't do it," said Dee, "the show can't go on!"

"This is all thanks to Jack," thought Sally, as she left the dressing room that evening to go and wait in the wings with the others. Poor old Jack the Lad! Banished for ever to the depths of Tara's pocket – well, until she found him there and threw him out, and who knew where that might be? It might be somewhere he would hate! Somewhere really boring. Somewhere lonely. She didn't like to think of Jack being lonely.

"'Scuse me," said Sally, suddenly turning and pushing her way past Martina.

"Where are you going?" hissed Shayna. "We're on in a few minutes!"

"I know. I won't be a second!"

Sally raced down the passage and into the dressing room. Tara's coat was hanging on the rail. She dipped her hand into the pocket and took out the pink pebble. Where could she put it? Somewhere safe, out of sight … high up, on the window ledge. That would do! A theatre was the right place for a ghost. He would enjoy himself there. He could haunt lots of famous people. There might even be other ghosts to talk to.

"Jack, be happy!" whispered Sally.

She was just going through the door when something caught her eye. She half turned. Slowly and shakily, across the dressing table mirror, a ghostly hand was spelling out a message:

Good luck Sally

The Door

by Gareth Owen

Gran thought I was going to die. I heard her whispering to the doctor. My temperature ran up to a hundred and four. I was thrashing about and talking all kinds of nonsense and crying for my mum. I sweated so much, my Gran had to change the sheets four times. "Enough sweat to float a ship," she said.

This was afterwards of course. At the time I didn't know what was going on. It was as if I wasn't there. I couldn't remember anything. When the doctor came, he said if the fever didn't break overnight, he'd call the hospital. Gran had to go to Mrs Simpson at the end of the Close to phone my mum. She told her I was ill but made out it wasn't serious. She didn't want to worry her.

Early the next afternoon the crisis seemed to have passed. When I opened my eyes I didn't know where I was at first. The whole room was turning round. At last it stopped and I saw Gran's worried face staring down at me. She brushed the wet hair out of my eyes. Her hand was cold on my forehead. She announced that I was much cooler. Later, she told me what had happened.

"I was watching you kick a tennis ball around in the cul-de-sac, when suddenly you stopped. You sort of spun round and then you went down like a sack of spuds. I thought you'd just fallen over at first, messing about. But when you didn't get up I knew that something was wrong. There was nobody about. I had to carry you in all on my own. You don't look much but you weighed a ton. Couldn't get you upstairs so I put you in my downstairs room."

I looked round at the double bed with the brass frame, the heavy old-fashioned curtains and the religious painting on the wall behind my head. Outside it was raining. Gran asked me if I remembered anything. I shook my head. The last thing I remembered was kicking this tennis ball against the wall. After that, nothing, but there was a large red bruise down my left arm.

Gran asked me if I wanted any broth. She was just going out to warm it up, when the doctor came again. He put the cold stethoscope on my chest.

"Ticker seems OK." He felt round my neck and then tapped my back. "Well, you're in better shape than yesterday. D'you remember yesterday?"

I shook my head.

"Lucky for you," he said smiling. "It was an awful day." He turned to Gran. "Well I think you can cancel the funeral arrangements for the time being. He's going to be right as rain. I should keep him in bed for a couple of days, just to be on the safe side."

He folded the stethoscope into his bag. "Remarkable recovery." He placed his hand on

Gran's shoulder. "Ah, youth, youth," he said sadly. "If that virus had hit you or me, we'd both of us be pushing up the daisies by now."

He snapped his bag shut. "I'll drop in again on Wednesday."

When he'd gone, Gran went round again to Mrs Simpson's to call my mum and tell her the good news. Even though I was weak, I could tell she was relieved. When she came back I could hear her singing in the kitchen, clattering pots and pans. I kept falling asleep and then waking up again. When I was awake, everything felt strange; as if I wasn't there somehow. As if I was somewhere else, watching myself.

It was funny lying in Gran's big double bed. They'd always slept downstairs. Grandad had been brought up in a farm cottage out at Stanmore. He'd never lived in a house that had an upstairs. He felt funny not sleeping near the ground so they'd built an extension and used it as a bedroom. After he died, Gran modernised the rest of the house but kept the bedroom as it had always been. It was like being in a museum. It didn't bother me though. Anyway I was too weak to care.

The floor was laid with brown linoleum and the walls were hung with these old black and white photographs; wedding pictures taken outside grey churches, with Grandad wearing spats. I recognised my mum in one of the photos. She must have been about my age at the time. I hadn't even been born then. It made me feel funny thinking about it.

One picture in particular caught my eye. It was a photo of a football team. Like in all team photographs, the players had their arms folded in the same way, left over right, and they were smiling straight at the camera. Compared with today, their boots looked ridiculously clumsy and heavy and their shorts were long and narrow. Two men in suits and waistcoats stood at the back, both with watch-chains looping from their waistcoat pockets. I guessed they were the manager and one of the directors. Although I still felt weak, I couldn't resist getting out of bed to take a closer look. I had to hold on to the brass bedstead to stop myself from keeling over.

The player in the middle at the front held one of those old-fashioned brown footballs in his hands. I suppose he must have been the captain. He stared seriously out at me. There was something written on the ball but it was too small to read. I picked up the magnifying glass from the bedside table. Peering through it, I finally made out the words on the ball: *Cup Winners 1937-38*.

Then a strange thing happened. As I stared at the picture, the faces began to shift and dissolve. I could have sworn the player holding the ball smiled and winked at me. I suppose it must have been the fever because my head started spinning again. The magnifying glass fell from my hand. If I hadn't leaned against the wall, I'd have fallen down.

"And who said you could get out of bed?" Gran had to half-carry me back to that big double bed. When I was tucked in and had eaten the broth she'd warmed up for me, I asked her about the photograph. There was something that worried me about it. She unhooked the photo from the wall and brought both it and the magnifying glass over. The photograph left a pale shape on the wall. Gran sat on a wicker chair beside the bed and stared at it with me. She sighed. "Best team City ever had," she said in a soft whisper. "I remember them all. Every one of them."

She pointed at a smiling stocky figure on the back row. His hair was thick and black and parted down the centre. "Smiler Bishop," she said, and she was smiling too as she remembered. "He was a character. If he tackled you, you had to count your legs after. And Lofty Chambers. He was the brains behind the team. Always looked as if he'd just got out of bed. Oh, he looked a mess! Smoked like a chimney. Always wore his sleeves over his fists. But from fifty yards he could drop a ball on a sixpence."

Her finger moved from one to the other as she repeated their names.

I pointed at the stern figure holding the ball. "What about him, Gran?"

She looked at me in surprise. "Don't you know who that is?"

I shook my head.

"That's your grandad. He was captain."

Looking closer, I could see the resemblance between him and the man in the wedding photo. "Grandad was the City captain?"

"Of course he was. They called him Chipper."

"Chipper? Why was that?"

"He was a carpenter by trade. Can't you tell?"

"No," I said.

"Have a closer look." She handed me the magnifying glass. I stared hard.

"Notice anything?"

I shook my head.

"His left hand."

Then I saw it. The third finger was cut off at the knuckle.

"Never knew a carpenter who had a full set of fingers," Gran said. She laughed. "Funny isn't it? 'Course, it weren't funny at the time. He was putting up a little garden shed at the back. That would be ... what?" She stared at the ceiling forcing her memory. "Thirty-six. The year the King abdicated. He was sawing away. It was a nice warm day. I was hanging out the sheets. We weren't long married. I was happy. Suddenly, the sawing stopped. He didn't shout or nothing. I looked over at him and he was staring at his hand with this blank look on his face. It was comical really. I said, 'What's up?'

"'Here Edie,' he said, 'you'll never guess what I've gone and done. Chopped me blooming finger off. Would you credit it?' And then he laughed." She shook her head sadly. "That was just like him."

I shifted my gaze from the missing finger to the frank, open, serious face. I was thinking, *that's my grandad.* There was something I didn't understand though. "If he was a professional footballer," I said, "how come he was a carpenter?"

"Ah well you see, it isn't like it is now with young lads getting all that money. In them days they got next to nothing. Twelve pound a week was all they got, although that was a lot more than other folks was getting then. So you needed a trade for when you hung your boots up for the last time. We couldn't afford a car. Didn't have a phone. Looking at the crowds that turned up every week, sixty, seventy thousand, I often wondered where all the money went. Into the directors' pockets I shouldn't wonder. They all had big houses out at Sheppey Common. A Rolls Royce in the drive. But Frank was never bitter. Wasn't his way. It's just how things were in those days. You accepted it. It seemed normal. He was happy just to be playing for the City. They didn't even lay on a taxi for him to the ground on match day. He used to catch the bus like everybody else.

"'All right, Chipper lad,' the fans would shout, and clap him on the back."

She tucked a stray strand of grey hair behind her ear. "I've known him and Smiler and Lofty kick a tennis ball around in the Close with a bunch of kids before a game. Put their bags down for a goal. I'd hear them from the kitchen, shouting and laughing and running about and the ball banging against the door. And the kids shouting out, 'Over here, Chipper. Shoot, Chipper.' "

For a moment Gran stared out of the window silently. "I can hear them now," she said softly.

"Hear them, Gran?"

She turned and smiled at me, pulled the sheets up to my chin and tucked me in. "Oh, in my mind," she said. "In my silly old woman's mind." She picked up the broth bowl. "Now enough of my memories, you try and get some sleep, Sonny Jim." She always called me Sonny Jim. I never knew why.

At the door she switched out the light. Just as she was closing the door, I remembered what it was I wanted to ask her.

"Gran, why are there crosses over the heads of three of the players?"

I could see her silhouette against the light in the hall. She didn't turn round. "Ah well," she said at last, "then the war came, didn't it." And she closed the door softly.

* * *

I must have slept all night and right through because when I woke up, the midday sun was streaming through the window. Everything was clear and steady. The walls of the houses gleamed like pearl. When they banged on the door I was able to get up straight away. My legs felt strong and my head was clear.

"Wakey, wakey, Sonny Jim," the voice called. When I opened the door I could see the three of them framed by the sunlight. I blinked in the light. The sky was like bruised white clay.

"Where you been, Sonny Jim?" said the soldier. He was sitting on the low garden wall. His khaki army beret was set on the side of his head and there was a small haversack at his feet. He stood up and stretched. "Got to get up earlier in the morning than this, Sonny Jim, if you want to score against the Arsenal. Ain't that right, Smiler?"

The two other soldiers were holding their berets in their hands and heading a tennis ball from one to the other. They laughed as they bobbed and ducked, their eyes squinting against the sunshine. The one called Smiler was smoking a cigarette. The smoke drifted up and across his face. He had one eye closed. "Fifty-five, fifty-six, fifty-seven," he chanted each time the tennis ball struck his forehead.

"Over here, Lofty lad," called Chipper, standing up suddenly and holding out both his arms. Lofty balanced the ball on his instep, then lobbed it across to Chipper, who trapped it expertly.

"Tell you what, Chipper," said Smiler, squeezing out his cigarette between finger and thumb and tucking it behind his right ear. "How about you and Sonny Jim there taking us on?"

"No contest," said Chipper, putting his arm round my shoulders. "We're an unbeatable combination ain't we, Sonny Jim?"

Lofty put the two haversacks down towards the end of the Close. "Your door's the other goal," he shouted.

Smiler walked up to us. "What about the rules?"

"What rules is that?" asked Chipper.

Suddenly, Smiler whipped the ball away from him, dribbled round me as if I wasn't there, and slammed the ball against the door frame and into my bedroom.

"The rule that says I score first," Smiler said, laughing.

I collected the ball from under the bed. There was a dark bruise on the brickwork surrounding the door. A rook flew low across the road and settled on the branch of a tree.

"Aw ref," Chipper said, holding out his arms, "we wasn't ready."

Smiler was shaking hands with Lofty. "Shock goal in the first second from the brilliant Smiler Bishop," he said in the voice of a commentator. I shook my head and laughed.

"Now then, Sonny Jim," Chipper said suddenly, passing the ball to me. He raced down the pavement, calling for it. I threaded it to him. He stopped. Feinted right, went left, then, using the garden wall, bounced it past Lofty before placing the return pass at my feet. Even I couldn't miss from there. I shot as hard as I could. The tennis ball struck the left-hand haversack, knocking it flat, before shooting away into somebody's garden.

"One-all," said Chipper, shaking my hand. "Got them on the run now, Sonny Jim."

I don't know how long the game lasted or who won or lost. But suddenly it was over. Chipper looked at his watch. He put his fingers to his lips and let out a shrill whistle. "Full-time lads." Then he tossed the battered tennis ball to me. I caught it.

"For next time," he said with a wink.

"Next time," I said.

He patted me on the head and turned to the other two. "Nearly kick-off time, lads."

Smiler clicked to attention like a sergeant major and shouted, "Get fell in you lads! The whistle has went!"

"Can't be late for this one, can we lads?" said Chipper.

They picked up their haversacks and put on their berets. I watched them sauntering down the Close. The sunlight blazoned them. At the end they turned and waved. "So long, Sonny Jim," they all shouted. I waved back.

And then they were gone, leaving me alone in the deserted Close. Even though I could no longer see them, I waved again and called softly after them, "So long, Smiler. So long, Lofty. So long, Chipper. So long."

* * *

I must have fallen asleep again and slept through the whole afternoon and night because, when I woke up, I could smell bacon frying and the sound of Gran's voice singing along to the radio. There was a dull ache at the back of my eyes and I felt thick with sleep. But I felt better.

"Well then, how's the patient?" Gran asked as I walked into the kitchen. She held a spitting frying pan in her hand: sausages, bacon, eggs and fried bread. "Thought you might like a proper breakfast."

She leaned forward and inspected me. "Well I must say you look better. The doctor was right. I think we can cancel the funeral."

I sat down at the table, rubbing my eyes. There was a pot of geraniums on the window sill and the sun threw a shaft of light across the red and white check table-cloth.

"Thought you was never going to wake up," Gran said. "Don't need to ask you if you slept all right."

"Well," I said. "I had a funny dream." And I told her about it. The three soldiers. The game we played. Smiler and his pranks. Chasing after the ball into the bedroom.

There was a crash as the frying pan fell from her limp hand and clattered onto the tiles. The fat leaked across the floor and the spilled eggs bled their yolks.

She was staring at me hard, her eyes wide. The blood had drained from her face. She swayed. For a moment I thought she was going to faint.

"You too," she whispered.

I stood up and took her arm. "What's the matter, Gran?"

Her voice was a hoarse whisper. "You're not the first. Hilda's lad saw them, too!"

"Gran," I said, "it was only a dream. That's all."

"Dream?" she said. "That was no dream."

"It must have been," I said. "I mean, there's no door there, is there?"

Her mouth opened and shut as if she wanted to say something but no words came out. She brushed her hand softly across my forehead, then she took my hand. I could feel her trembling. Without saying anything, she led me outside and round the front until we were standing outside the blank wall of the room where I'd slept the night before.

"Dream!" she said. "Dream?" She pointed at the wall. "Look," she said. "Look there."

I followed her pointing finger. In the faded brickwork was a faint outline in older bricks. And the outline, unmistakably, was in the shape of a door.